I0762505

Raven on the Moaners' Bench

Also by Gary Copeland Lilley

The Subsequent Blues

Alpha Zulu

High Water Everywhere

The Bushman's Medicine Show

Chapbooks:

The Reprehensibles

Black Poem

Cape Fear

The Hog Killing

Raven on the Moaners' Bench

poems

Gary Copeland Lilley

Four Way Books
Tribeca

For

my siblings
Bradford Mizell Lilley
Cynthia Vanessa Lilley-Denson
Jeffrey Iraton Lilley
Lorraine Regina Lilley
Gay Patricia Lilley-Spellman

and our mother
Lillian Camilla Copeland Lilley
who raised us all
inside the church of her love

and Tess

Library of Congress Cataloging-in-Publication Data

Names: Lilley, Gary, author.
Title: Raven on the moaners' bench : poems / Gary Copeland Lilley.
Description: Tribeca : Four Way Books, 2025.
Identifiers: LCCN 2025003849 (print) | LCCN 2025003850 (ebook) |
ISBN 9781961897625 (trade paperback) | ISBN 9781961897632 (ebook)
Subjects: LCGFT: Poetry.
Classification: LCC PS3612.I42 R38 2025 (print) | LCC PS3612.I42 (ebook)
| DDC 811/.6--dc23/eng/20250207
LC record available at https://lccn.loc.gov/2025003849
LC ebook record available at https://lccn.loc.gov/2025003850

This book is manufactured in the United States of America and printed on acid-free paper.

Four Way Books is a not-for-profit literary press. We are grateful for the assistance we receive from individual donors, public arts agencies, and private foundations including the New York State Council on the Arts, a state agency.

We are a proud member of the Community of Literary Magazines and Presses.

Contents

Raven on the Moaners' Bench

Da/Loco/Mojo *(What Can Drive You Crazy)*

Raven on the Moaners' Bench

Prelude

The first pew in the old-time
black church is the Moaners' Bench.
It is empty, waiting for those
who will come forward during the service
asking to be saved.
The term "moaners" comes from
their audible expressions
of spiritual need, of bodily reaching
toward the lifting away,
the forgiveness of the heavy
burden of their sins.
There is also a feeling of joy coming
from the whole congregation
because of that forgiveness.

Moaners' Bench

I can't tell you the why
or how my dead younger brother
died long before he actually did
on those shameless roads
and stretch-marked streets
edging the hateful soul
of the southern border states
it seems nobody
realizes what hides in
the dangerous beauty
of deserts or a 200-foot wave
of a hurricane on the ocean
or how much trouble there is
for the community near or under
the tracks he lived
almost to retirement age
and I being seven years older
my everything is still what will fit
inside my social security check
and my seabag that's
the meager way I have lived
I should tell you I know
plenty family and friends
that are now gone

and I wonder why
I am not dead
in my brother's place
or put down beside him
where he was against
a wilderness of hope
brought back to our
birthplace and we could
finally come to him
as the one we always loved
but could never have him back
except as ashes, ashes
and memory.

“Thou Shalt Not Be Afraid for the Terror by Night”

from Psalm 91

The night my younger brother
was hit by the car, the driver
was a drunk running through
the red light,

a drunk running through a red light,
redlight, redlight:
the driver, the car, a drunken red light—

police determined that before the strike
the drunk never even touched his brakes,
never tapped the brakes,

punk-ass motherfucker pump the brakes
motherfucker never touched the goddam brakes.

in the red light my younger brother
standing dead in the crosswalk—
the impact took his 6-foot-5 frame,
took him through the front windshield,

breaking glass, breaking bone,
banging through metal

and out the back windshield,
landing twisted,

twisted all up, twisting-the-night-away
in the still moving road, moving
with cars and people walking—

did anyone come to me
in that glare and pitch
of me out of one kind of life
and into a life where the street
was all I had, that and whoever
else had ended up there not knowing
why, but still there

and eventually on the street
where we would never again
meet in the never-of-no-goodbyes,
just a slow unseen knowing
he was out there somewhere
living in-the-no-goodbye-
wide-open-way he accepted
his world broken
day by broken day.

"Nor for the Arrow That Flieth by Day"

from Psalm 91

He woke from the two-month coma,
all his bones broken,

the broken bones had knitted wrong
and had to be rebroken;

he was 19, and the subsequent
schizophrenia when it hit
musta covered him like a blanket—wait,
hell naw, like sheet lightning,
everything lit up all at once,
and all his communication options
buzzing and accelerating.

He was screaming that shit but says
it musta been somebody else yelling
because he wasn't even here,
so therefore couldn't possibly
have said anything like that.

But he was very much there,
I heard him say it and thrash
his words at all of us,
his family who loved him

yet could not reach him,
shattered in his suit of fire
and reaching past us, wired
the way the sun is to the moon
and spills every which way, never
to be contained again.

"Nor for the Pestilence That Walketh in Darkness"

from Psalm 91

It was like this, a dark day, a dark day,
a day dark with storm when everyone
sits quiet in the kitchen because God
is speaking, but my dead younger brother
spoke because he didn't have any quiet,

no quiet, I had no quiet in my head or
anywhere else, no quiet.

Not a quiet boy like he used to be.
He told my sanctified mother that God
didn't save him when he was dead in a coma,
couldn't have saved him; he insisted
on death, his very own death
as only he could know it, so it must have been,
it had to have been the devil's hand,
he claimed, that brought him back:

Devil lift me right out of death,
ain't no trouble to him,
he's good at beating God to you every time.

It was then he had to leave us,
it was then he had to leave

my mother's house,
and my mother loved him, he
was hers, and of her
but she was afraid of the darkness
of his demon, she was sorrowful afraid
of his demon, afraid of the roaring
she felt she could hear of his demon and
although she knew it was his,
his demon, how could she be sure
it wouldn't come, wouldn't
walk among her household, tear
at the sanity of her grip on
a godly world and her passage
through it—not with a demon,
not living with one, her beloved
son who believed he had been
saved by a demon, and left
to wander, enduring the world—
continual eviction—where no mother
could take him in.

When My Dead Younger Brother Left, My Little Sister Was Glad

He started pissing, she said, pissing
down the walls and in the corners,
and he'd hock up to spit on the floor
of whatever room he was standing in

mind your own damn business I stand
when gnashing my dinner in the kitchen,
if I want to eat standing up, I stand up

at least he got up from the table,
he didn't do that anywhere else,
in the living room he would stretch that
crooked left leg and turn
towards the wall with his "self"
in one hand, TV remote in the other
and piss the carpet like something wild.

He barked his orders at my mother
like a hellhound, she said, at my mother.
Yes Lord, pacing through the house
he scared the heaven right out of them.
They never had the escape of sleep,
not one solid damn night,
not one gentle night of sleep.

My Dead Younger Brother, What Can Kill You?

And then there's the difficulties
in not getting enough rest,
in not losing your medicines,
in not eating well, not staying clean,
your feet wearing calluses
and wrong shoes walking beneath you.
Not staying warm and dry
in the winter and with less than
Holy treatment on the menu,
being with a busload of young convicts
carrying invisible long sentences,
and there's always, damn right, that kind
of rotten "always" of bad-apple police.

My Dead Younger Brother Believes He Is a Missionary Baptist

There once was a time that Asheville
was the place where true believers
administered to the less fortunate
right in the middle of town: soups,
bread and healthcare in the Pritchard Park
triangle where the drummers send up
messages to God every Friday night
until the snows come. Some folks
say my dead younger brother
was there looking for Jesus
and some say that he *was* Jesus,
what the hell do they know about that,
huh, huh, what the hell do they know?
If he was Jesus he might still
be chasing the money lenders out
of the temples or walking on
everyday tap water or swamp water
or clear as avalanche lake water
or any whiskey-colored
river water and I could walk to him
out there in the middle
of the French Broad River, walk
that water and give him
something real to do like lead me

back to shore and steady me up
with his loaves-and-fishes ways,
with his come unto me all ye little
children—and like the child I was
when we were children together
we'd take each other's hand
and be brothers and be just those
very children beside
that river, that walkable
ever-flowing river.

What It's Like to Live With a Lack of Shade

I had left home for college, but
told my dead younger brother
that all the high school boys back home
go to Wildwood, New Jersey
like I had done because I never planned
on doing another hot summer
of farm work, there ain't but so much fun
you can have on a tractor,
working the crop on the endless
and shade-less furrows—
the whole eastern side of North Carolina
seemed to be just one big damn farm
of cotton or corn or peanuts
and eventually that can kill you.
And not even eventually but
the way a nothing-there-for-you
can burrow into you and
dark-you-in like a secret eclipse
no one can find a way to prove,
it could slam a planet, a person,
in the broad daylight, and my
brother, who because he died
younger than he even actually
died, took my older-brother advice

and packed his two favorite
Kool & the Gang t-shirts and whatever
he valued from the nightstand
and got himself for hire in Wildwood
where his back didn't blaze
with sun and peel in the dark
and what he did in the daytime
didn't rob the fun out of his
teenage New Jersey nights.

A Memory My Dead Younger Brother Gave to Me

When he was a teen working the summer
in Wildwood with a bunch of his friends,
they rented the same house that me
and my friends had lived in six years earlier,
next door to Cecelia who was pregnant
when I met her, and would be
my girlfriend that summer:
we read books silently and to each other,
smoked menthol cigarettes
and weed, and it felt good to lay with her
when I came home in the morning
from the midnight crew at Michael's Bakery
(where my dead-younger would also find a job).
Cecelia, my sprinkle of cinnamon in a cup of coffee,
we had multiple break-ups and make-ups,
O God how I loved being with her
that summer before I was drafted into the army.
And it was for you no aftermath, not
for me nor her, my brother,
that another shower of blessings fell to you,
and like leaving Cecelia, was a kind of incidental
joint sanity we both lost by leaving, not only her,
but the young way we had of thinking this
one minute then something else the next—

each of us for a precious while giving
ourselves over to her as if she was
ourselves in a better more loving form
with shatterings of laughter and delight,
in our daylight and moonlight. Only now
I'm glimpsing this because you have left it,
not for good, but only as memory
allows us to leave even those
most precious to us, who held even us,
who were beyond wisdom and time,
are held for any moment's chance
at eternity, that provisional heaven
of the both of us.

My Dead Younger Brother and Folding Money

When he was in middle school,
some of the old black farmers
were still driving mule carts,
click-clock steel shoes on the blacktop
going to the store at the crossroads
to buy a plug of tobacco, a can of snuff
or a cold coke-cola; those old farmers
in the rural south would wave
to every yard or porch that had people
sitting in the shade who also lifted
a waving hand towards them,
and the tractors and pick-up trucks
gunned their motors past the mules
to Jake Stallings' Store where my
dead younger brother pumped gas
for anyone he thought had a dollar
to give; he was always smiling
and for that I called him Nickles
(I honestly can't tell you why
because it was always folding money,
nobody paid him with change).
What did I see then about money,
and working for it, that I had to forget
when you kept working beyond the daily

indignities of those Jim Crow jobs
where we squandered our young
irreplaceable days—and when I could
I said no, sat on a shady porch
and waved when the mule carts
clattered past. Just one hand raised
signaled a forest of understanding.

My Dead Younger Brother Thumbing Through the South

He got 90 days in Florida for vagrancy—
for being black and a stranger walking
through Kissimmee with less than twenty dollars.
He never said exactly but I do believe
he was repeatedly fighting for his manhood
in the prison because after his
incarceration he consumed women
with a desperate need.
After 90 days on the road-gang
they released him at the brick courthouse
in the middle of Kissimmee
with not one dollar in his pocket.
He run clean out of that town
and went west on Highway 40
through Arkansas, Texas, Arizona
to California until he couldn't go further
(he probably would have swam
to Japan if he knew how to swim).
I hope I gotta prayer to give,
one I really don't need like a shot
of high-proof rye to keep me warm
or like a necessary tool discovered
by accident and need on a Swiss Army knife
for a man in the miles of encampments

on the thin shoulders of Highway 10
as you come into Pomona.
Every time I work down to my last
twenty dollar bill I stash it
in my mind's memory pocket
so you, my brother, work free all the days
of your westward life, this encampment
on the way to the rumor you followed
from Sandy Cross, a lot of it on foot
to the slow lapping slip-back waters
of the suddenly-shining-before-you Pacific.

Black Hopperesque Night Scene

for Jeff

You missed my American journeys, Jeff,
while under pressure of your own.

I can say living night and day as practically
the only black man in this touristy

shipbuilding town is maybe farther
than any cry could join us. But let me

tell you a cop story, of which you had plenty.
The anti-hero of mine is the same cop

that has stopped me six times already,
and you of all people, you will believe me.

I say it again so you feel the way he marked
me, yes there are only four black men

driving these Victorian streets: me and
another guitar player, and two others

I am grateful for but have never
had the occasion to know. Remember

I went to sea while you were also at sea
in your own way. Anyhow, to fill

you in, I'm a veteran, a retired teacher
who goes out at night to play guitar

at Uptown Bar and Grill. I drive
a junebug green '94 Cadillac Sedan DeVille

because I dig all that space, the heated seats,
seats radiating under my ass. This cop

followed me at midnight. I am saying midnight, Jeff,
and I know you have the chill of this, shadowed

at that exact hour, being followed at midnight
he scared the shit outta me because he

was clocking me from a parallel street with all
his lights off so I drove straight to Safeway

Supermarket which is open 24/7 and lit up
like a chicken factory any hour of that 24.

Without running I hurried into a store that
was almost empty, but from the deli section

I peeped the cop scanning aisles looking
for me. I bought a soggy roast beef sandwich,

a bag of salt and vinegar chips, a ginger ale,
smiled nicely at the who-cares-who-you-are

sleepy cashier and ambled leisurely to my car,
noticing the cop sliding into his cruiser.

I chose to sit in that diffuse parking lot light
and drink my cold soda because if I went

back out on the street, Jeff, we know he would
find a place, the very place, to stop me

and taking his given moment, the one I can't keep
from arriving, just when it will arrive, he will do

as I expect, as any of us black men would,
that he'll lift his gun and shoot, whenever

I see him *he's always seen me first.*

Hunger

Jeff, I want to tell you about a doe
in a Northwest pathway of my own
migration, far from our Southern roots
and hoodoo wizardries that kept us
some sort of alive for generations
when failing to edge our way around
white fears and hate which could be
certain death which I am allergic to
and you've got to be, too, riding
your thumb across highway and bog
through North Carolina, then to Texas
and California traveling with Helen.
But, back to this doe. I was leaning
into the cliff drop, a madrone, me
on the edge gazing into the valley.
She claimed my passage as pure
beings can, a yearling lying gutted
and strewn across the trail near
a snarl of wild pink rhododendron.
A cougar-kill. I could clearly see her,
and I'm on this page trying to write
a good poem for her, and to tell you, Jeff,
her delicate unbeauty in death, my wanting

just to touch her, to feel her before she
was taken down, and me standing
right over her, unable to see anything
beyond her eviscerated body, her chest
cavity bloodied, ravaged through,
that long strip of muscle at the backbone—
the tenderloin gone, stomach, heart,
the lungs, and her wide empty clutch of ribs
eaten right into the dirt, emptying me out, as she
was emptied out. Yet I tell you, brother,
she was there where she fell out of any return
but this—so I can tell you, who was often
cougar-hungry and who simply walked it
to your next oblivion, swallowed it down
fangs and claws, where hunger lives
in its hallowed privacy of killing and being
killed in unwitnessed silence. And to you
who didn't kill anything with your hunger
I offer up the sacrifice of one doe sprawled
in the what-was-left-of-her on the pathway
where I had to meet her and bring her away
to show you I understood something of how
you bore a terrible cost for our family,

for this unholy country, a cost for which
I won't allow any repayment
by words, not mine or anyone's,
on any unstained page.

A Prayer in Four Parts to See if God Is Still Listening

1.

He often wondered about that to me,

> *do you think he's really still listening?*
> *can you hear his listening inside you?*

How can a brother, even an older
brother answer him when he says
he's of the devil but still wants
and cares whether God listens or not?
Of course, I wrote him a prayer, even
if he never gets to read or hear me say it.
A man, a brother like that with the devil
at his back and God left to his own devices
needs at least one answered prayer,

> *wouldn't kindness and blood allow it?*

2.

If a powerline of crows is a murder
is a canopy of seagulls our jury?
Everyone wants the best *Good-Googa-Mooga*,

we cannot wait to make it our own. I want
the best for my brother, alive and dead.
We look to the hills for our help, O Lord,
our strength and redeemer, our
vaccinator, O Lord, of the unemployed—

is there shelter in a time of storm?

3.

All things are activated through my servitude,
mercy not just to others, but also to myself.
Should not love inspire us all—
hard times swarm, a nest of angry wasps,
but when the good news comes we sing
hallelujahs, dear God, dear God,

should I have to talk in tongues?

4.

Lord, may you rapture us away from the temple steps
and the grocery stores like you do for the dazed man
my dead younger brother is, in his ragged

clothes waiting for the Christ,
and the sign he holds saying it all—
"Lord Help Me," a woman in blue passes him
bread through the window of her bashed-fender Subaru,

> *did you do that, Lord, just like that,*
> *hand it over at the light, just like that?*

My Dead Younger Brother Knows What Love Is

When he says, *I know what love is made of*:
he means those sometimes experiences
that are outside, outside, way-the-fuck
outside of the reality that is of a mind
paranoidly maintained (like a living room
with plastic on couches and chairs) but
a mind with thoughts that might not exhibit,
might not show, might not point you
to a disorganization of behavior,
the tell-tale disruptions of his language,
what I mean is, sometimes those thoughts
can seem normal; let's say you are black
and hoboing in Texas, let's say you
feel safe, safe, safe and protected, fierce,
strong as two-weeks' unwashed armpits,
then maybe that safety is love, so when
he finds, he says, a black woman that wants
the same safety and agrees to be with him,
a woman named Helen in the dark at a bend
of a river in Texas, and he lays himself down
beside her, even if I tell you what I know
everybody said, I'm talking family now,
that they really didn't—Helen and my dead
younger brother—they really didn't love

each other. But he says, *me and Helen,*
me and Helen, he says, *we crossed*
America together, and one way or
another, he says, *we been together*
thirty years, and ain't that something,
brother? Is it, ain't that something, is it,
that sure is something ain't it?
SShhhh, that question, he says, *doesn't*
require anybody's answer only
Helen and me lived the answer
and won't nobody else involved
so shut the fuck up assholes,
it's just me and Helen.

My Dead Younger Brother Does Divination

If the card turned is Jack of Hearts
reversed, I'm bound to tell
an old man that if it comes to him,
or others that will grab a woman
by her love handles, then loose-talk
about it, those drunk-ass gray-stubbled
motherfuckers, bottle-in-the-pocket
motherfuckers in the logwoods
of worry, chainsaw broken with age
old men that come to the conjurer
about this problem: no man wants
to outlive the propaganda of his dick,
or wants to slip into disgrace
and to see himself flaccid between
the sheets on any woman's bed,
no man wants to outlive his dick.
So go 'head turn one more card,
maybe it'll inspire your root, unless
you the one that talks too much.
Turn that card.

Road Disappears in California for My Dead Younger Brother

There he is, there he is, he is there,
my dead younger brother
on the street of lost and angels
where every night he unrolls
his sleeping bag in a different place;
the white kids, white kids
from the suburbs, the white kids
setting fire to the homeless,
spray lighter fluid, lighter fluid
on the instantly flammable homeless
if they appear to be drunk,
appear to be stoned or addled
and I worry 'cause at any time,
any time, at any time
my brother could be all three.

It was at a bend in a river,
at a river in Texas he found Helen
sleeping on the ground—
they've been married at least
thirty years and they really don't,
don't really love each other some say
but feel safer, safer, safer together.

And who says that isn't
the heart of love, and whose
heart can you actually
speak for but your own
unseeable, non-accountable
wavering crisscross heart,
saying something stupid about
what obviously is, I mean,
right out here in plain sight
about two black human beings
who cleaved to each other,
in the cold and poverty
of midnights on a road
going out of sight under them
in kill-you-any-minute-
as-easy-as-look-at-you
present-day America.

We Just Need to Know He Loves Helen from Troy

A gray light had left a depression
in him, rain flooded his mental ditch,
mud washed through his opened mouth—
a drowning dreamed nightly of going
to some fast-food place, some shop,
some apartment, and coming out
not knowing where he was because
nothing was the same and he couldn't
get back to where he came from,
and in the dream he couldn't remember
who he was, and that's why he needs
Helen, 'cause brain-cramp is a daily
experience, the only thing he could
really hear other than the Texas twang
of her voice were the voices in his head
he believes are God, Jesus, the Disciples,
and the New Orleans Saints.

Bow-wow-yo-yippy-yay, his road dawgs
from under the tracks singing
a big black guy is looking for Jeff
and since they don't know this searcher
they deny any knowledge of him:

now isn't that what one disciple did to Jesus
three times before the rooster crowed,
it was our brother Brad searching
and finding him two days later
by the railroad tracks, and then Jeff
wonders why Brad is there,
in a West Hollywood hallucination
and not North Carolina, but there he is,
real as dirt, real as the work boots
that he put on Jeff's now size 14 feet,
real as the cigarettes he gave him,
wanting him to come back home
in these woe-be-gone days,
the home he knew now existed.

Family is real, but Jeff wanted
Brad to know, for some indiscernible
reason, that Helen's from Troy, Texas
and she crazy as hell but she ain't
as crazy as Jeff is, she knows
he's loved her calendars of years,
full days of minutes and moments
that are the light he lives by, O Helen

Full Jar of Grease, she loves him but
when he's off his meds he's mister nasty,
a pornographic son-of-a-bitch and those
are the times she won't be around him.
She checks on his wellbeing and tells him
he should at least be sober like she is
at times is, before his health fails again;

she done seen him through Covid and
pneumonia and nursed him through
a drug stroke and makes sure he eats
at least once a day and that love shows
you the real truth, that love is why
he can't leave this place, even when
the draw is family and maybe
being warm and fed is a certainty,
and they know you from blood,
in the blood I'm saying, which tempts
you, in a fierce way, could claim you.
But Helen, nobody mentioning a place
for her and if there is no place for Helen
how can there be a place for him?
And he ain't going nowhere

without Helen, without her love,
which is as sure as he'll ever be
about anything in the very blood
that carries him.

Raven on My Fence the Day of My Brother Jeff's Memorial

I don't know the way out of these woods,
this sad day of the pandemic when
we are not allowed to gather—in this
unkindness a raven 'lights a fencepost
and watches the porch and looks
into my kitchen at me at the table
with my computer as I zoom
into the North Carolina ceremony.

How do I mourn him like my mother
was doing before her death; do I wail
for someone who was already absent?
Someone we had not talked about,
someone I had not seen in fifty years?

But when a sibling dies you are never the same:
learning he is dead changes my world,
changes me in ways I didn't expect.
I'm afraid of what I've never
feared before, the void illuminated.
There he is. Jeff. No other sign is needed.

What message does the raven bring
from the spirit world? His arrival

brings me comfort; souls travel on wings,
magic from the world where Jeff is now.
This raven brings peace and a hive
of family spirits, let me light a candle. Lord,
let me light one candle.

I wanted all of us to live forever,
but I am shown we will not,
the raven on my fencepost sends
his steel-eyed look, sends
and receives love, the light
that reaches where his going
takes us, carries us out of here
on our black wings.

Da/Loco/Mojo *(What Can Drive You Crazy)*

Absolution

I ain't never lived in Eden, but
understand that I know Snake,

consider I see where he's coming
from, that he's got angel knowledge

of the surface and brings his bright
light to the underworld;

some of us who are born deep
into that hiss-side of the tracks:

where we from, everything's a swallow
of high-proof moonshine with storms

stirred in; there are troubles
and trials, a newspaper load; but

on the garden side the sun shines
blessings down on every ass there,

and the lush grasses carpet their
naked feet, and they ain't never

worried; they believe they been given
this privilege from God, who Snake

also loves and serves with all his
cold-blooded heart; he naturally

feels he deserves better treatment,
of course he resents them, his kind

ain't mild-mannered like those animals
that graze God's bountiful garden.

His kind, fitted out with teeth,
deep-rooted, tangled underground

enough to know that you can reach
anywhere by the crooked road

and that is more than an advantage,
that is the way there without

the way back which is only going
and going some more on what

nobody gave you for free.
Give me nothing, and I will give you

the uncertain good of it dug out of this
uncertain earth, a wild and penitent heart,

'cause I ain't never been to Eden.

Surviving Through the Sabbaths

God is our banjo-playing blues man,
our theoretical back-pocket bottle—
in the cold hard rain we will rise
warm and dry, you'll hear a wailing train
in the distance, magnify Him and you will find
the red words, holy merciful water sprinkled
in the lit alleys of your unanswerable prayers,
the ones God loves because they give him back
his unreasonable mandates to love
the unlovable beyond the furthest misery,
and to do it like the bird who picked up
his wings and flew, and who didn't care
if it was the sky or the wings
that did the flying, the whole narcotic
of sky just being a heaven of inexplicable
and unknowable dimension,
being plenty and enough to tame a sabbath,
this one gracious day of any
work-killed week.

Blue Moon Ramble

slow blues fits like a crow
perched in a crooked tree

folks ask why am I so
sad why don't I try to sing love
songs and I say if I were to
sing a love song it ain't
necessarily gonna be too
happy because love can
become sad and those
songs lean heavy on that

*

woundwort spreads
into meadows
and slides down hillsides
like rambunctious children's
run-together summer days
of rural-Carolina-coast

swamp mosquitos swarm
in the tall grass

*

run-away to MamaDaisy's
a place we called "the railroad"
one mile through the woods
where the tracks had been removed
now just a game trail
that exits at the blacktop
and the safety of her

she's mending at the kitchen table
my chair in the woodstove's warmth

*

summer is two months' farm work
in shade-less fields
the calluses long gone
but cat in the sun look
look how old my hands
are today
the branches of creases
latticework
around swollen knuckles

the fingernails
chewed to the quick

*

a man whose voice
was beer bottles
being dashed in the road
his wife's voice
when he was home

shattered dishes
swept across a kitchen floor

*

we sit in the bucket seats of the car
at Hillcrest in the reflected glow
of red and blue neons blinking
in the bar's long windows
and the slow-dance music from inside

buzzes like a honeybee
hums like a mosquito

*

at the jukebox the girl I danced with
we always did our wobble
the finger-pop the slide the kick

our-dirty-Sandy-Cross-represent
we retired in different states of being
never stayed in touch

if she remembers any song on that jukebox
then we're still dancing together

*

last call   a celebration
to the remainder of this night,
the music in my head and heart
a bucket of cool water deep in the well
of flirtations   the pungency of stains

everything that declares a person
is on the upside of alive

*

MamaDaisy's wake
a mourning wreath hangs
on her front door
I step from the porch
into the living room where
the collective grief

is like an underground river
meted out upon me

sorrow spoonful by
spoonful

*

I am 12 when I tell
MamaDaisy I don't want to be
in anybody's world
if she wasn't in it

she smiles and kisses me
on my forehead

(This Is) Belvidere, NC

This is who the rural black folks are:
the Superintendent of Sunday School,
it is believed that, at her age, with
her title, her faith, she's synonymous
with Saint, a full moon of backwoods
opulence, a blackwater swamp
that promises a continual catfish stew.
Almost twenty years it has been
since my mother came back down here
from New York to live, and now she is dying,
she's been dying for some time and
here she is, eighty-four and proud beneath
one of her regal church crowns
behind the leather-covered steering wheel
of her harvest-gold Grand Marquis.
I figured out that she's racing me down
the road when we're both driving to church.
A low-ground-blessing-of-liberation
is the power of an old woman driving
her own car that she paid for
with her own money; she knows that
and gives her keys to no one, not even me—
the boy down the road who cuts her grass
every Saturday makes sure her sedan

looks free from sin on Sundays—
he rubs that metal until it squeals
like Gabriel's saxophone
and it's a holy transformation, parked
in sanctified sunlight.

…and the Avenging Angel Appeared

They say there was a lilt
in the voice of the woman
reading the future headline
to the battered wife
saying her husband had been
kicked out of his face
a wide wedge of jawbone was
found on a trail he'd been walking
up in the Olympic Mountains—
they say it must have been
a spirit from way back that
came down on him
tired of being hurt and scorned
she drew herself up and became
the Angel of the Lord
and the first thing she said
to relieve the soon-to-be-widow
was honey do not be afraid
sit down with your coffee
take it easy   making remnants
out of assholes like him
is just what I do.

Ars Poetica

Language chock full of music, a dance
of words I am just hearing
in the very moment I presently reside,
a direct correlation 'cause I arrived
as a mute child, my voice-bat ricocheting
in the cage of my head,
drumbeats from four hundred years ago
spired to bloom a prophet-weed
counter to my enslaved hyphenations,
my unexpected clicks and stammers,
the old-school skipping-needle stuck
on my cracked vinyl—this is a world
that wants to rake my tongue
from its river-bottom truths; with its scars
and throat catchments, this lost-way-mapping
inflicted on me as switchback head-howls,
an accumulation of forced silences,
hesitations that-that-that were rendered
by the drumbeats that delivered me
to an unkindness of ravens
dressed in their blackhearted best.

Da/Loco/Mojo *(What Can Drive You Crazy)*

All sorts of almost-truths attributed to him:
somebody said his favorite spiritual office
was in the yard under the giant Mulberry
and he had an iron roundtable,
and a comfy seat where they couldn't see him
but he could see everything,
including his garden of healing herbs,
the hoodoo house he really lived in.
This world is relentless, sharp
teeth filed and ready to chew
through gristle: he has a good friend
of long standing whose regular
greeting was *hey dude, what,*
you still among the living?
She'd say it with affection, no harm
intended. One day he told her
that shit gives him bone chills
and she needed a new opening line,
his point being folks aren't aware
of the power of the mouth,
that the world's voracious appetite
is not to taste us
but to swallow us whole.

Morning from the Wheelchair Lady at the Newsstand

That dark-skin girl from Haiti/they say she twenty year old/you know her/she was killed/in the broad daylight/we going about minding each our own damn business/whole bunch of people in a crowd/but mostly women waiting for the 7:20 bus/it's shame to us all/she got stabbed look like a dozen times/everyone there watching scared/could do not a thing/the blade flash/the blood flying and today/that girl is no more/after she stabbed by this no-kind-a-man/he want to marry her/he say/what so now/why waste time/we all seen him/killing her/that dark-skin girl who works at the dry-cleaner/on Patterson Avenue/she got a baby girl/they say is not none of his/now we see him on TV news/walking goddamn puffed-up proud/in chains like he Big-Big King Rude-Boy Bad-Ass/they know he the one/can't they just kill dead this man/what investigation needed now/it is over/girl dead/as she was the moment he drive a knife/through her heart/do not waste another damn minute/kill him during a commercial break/stab him/many times and times over/stab him so blood just run/like he did that pretty Haitian girl.

Collage: House for Sale

Three gnarled and twisted dogwoods two pear trees
Clamor and rioting and fierce turbulence of whiskey
Flower-beds out front fighting through weeds
Dressed-up man the twenty suits still in the closet
Rack of silk ties hanging inside the bedroom door
Waterlogged hardwood floors a family once lived here
Flannel shirt and military camouflage field jacket
Oil and dirt on work boots and wrinkled khakis
Sink full of dirty dishes Bible on the kitchen table
A one-armed doll a box of abandoned toy trucks
Closet with scattered blouses and dresses and scarves
Last year's garden stray beans and feral stalks of corn

Migration of My Negro Family

for love of James Baldwin

Hit that rhythm on the drum,
the rhythm you born with,
eternal Jim Crow can't douse
fire in a woodstove, my grandma
baking our biscuits every morning,
she raised her children, regulated
heat, her peg-legged husband gone,
Smith & Wesson .38 snub-nose
tucked in the waistband, a logging
road beside a lazy blackwater river,
blind uncle sitting on a cypress stump
listens to his hounds sing as they run,
and knows each by its bray, the holler
where the moonshine is made,
the juke joints replaced by rap videos
from Memphis, Atlanta, the swamp
of the Carolina coast and cousins
up north doing a beaded dance
with shekeres, the old folk pray
and testify in storefronts, the big brick
church on the same street, struggle-up
stay-awake altar boys assist the pastor
in preparation for communion, drugs
pass hand to hand even on Sundays,

any one of us jumping turnstiles
in subway stations, flirting in the dark,
a string of cowrie shells and prayers
that no more of us would die
on busted tail-light traffic stops, going
to rural and urban segregated schools,
one parent works in a noisy factory,
one works spacious white folks' kitchens
basting the yardbird with olive oil
and herbs, and another prays
her young mister gets a good job,
drives cab or sells insurance, becomes
a mortician, or gets a scholarship,
maybe teach at the college, or is called
towards the holy word of God when she
hears it in the hand-carved drums
at Prospect Park, all of it home
in the trees, in the heart-beat:
I know it was the blood saved me ...

Choices for My Mother's Ceremony

I gave you that revolver, my hand
to your hand gave it weight,
the H&R combat .22; you loaded
the cylinder, cocked the hair-trigger,
and gangsta-style sideways put
that dark barrel to his drunk head
and told him it might be best he just
leave you alone, you a bad Mamma-Jamma
for making him finally hear you—but
excuse me mom, I got side-tracked;
Brat's righteously leading us,
we do the things we know that you
want us to do, he prays and takes care
of all of us, he does not let us worry;
Sis chose your pink skirt-suit,
white silk blouse, and we know
that funeral homes don't want
nobody wearing shoes in the casket,
fearing that maybe you'll get up
and walk, I bet that'll get everybody's
attention huh; I got a quiet pair
of black pumps in case they
will put them on you for an extra
hundred; an assortment of your bling

I'll make sure goes with you,
silver bangles on both wrists,
a sapphire brooch needle-threaded
into your lapel, and your hair-do,
it's done nice old-school Oshun—
you gonna bless the church house,
all our wet eyes in it, and that pistol,
Dear Mother, it comes back to me.

Ars Poetica

They are all there, as she is, under
the angel—the graveyard's
hundred-year-old oak that lost
a limb the last windstorm.
It still throws a warm shade on her.
I keep all their graves free of weeds
when home, I play the djembe for them.
Uncle Bear smoked (remember, he would
scratch his back on the door frame)
so I put a thick cigar by his stone.
His children have gone north
so I do this for them. Maybe someone
will read a poem for childless me,
or splash some bourbon and a gospel song?
But on this, my mother's birthday, there's
wisteria. She loves wildflowers,
the purple unseasonal blooming vines
at the edge of the woods,
just before you step
                    into the cemetery.

When the Weight Comes Down

My advice, just keep quiet, shut
your mouth and become a loblolly pine
swaying in the distance, no matter
if you always felt like a shack
with blistering paint and a crooked
chimney in the middle of nowhere
from a long time ago, but perhaps
in this parable you live in High Point,
and your neighborhood was across
the invisible railroad tracks, or maybe
across the actual tracks where whatever
parent(s) you had and their parent(s) too,
worked as a furniture factory laborer
maybe with a missing index finger
and still running a bandsaw or assembling
dinette chairs or rolling a forklift
of freight to the loading dock and
maybe one of them had seen some
sad matriarch's grandson get shot
in Matthew Johnson's liquor-house
on a Friday night, the smell of fish-grease
coming from the kitchen, maybe a tumbler
of bourbon and ice on the card table,
a fresh supposedly unmarked deck

just out the box, a long-legged gal
standing behind is rubbing herself
into his back like his fresh money
waiting for her, maybe an unlit
fat reefer hanging off his bottom lip
makes a lop-sided smile, a fancy watch
on his wrist, and his hands—
gold rings flashing his shuffle—
hands busy pulling a pile of lost
rents toward him all night, maybe
a desperate car title temptingly
tossed into the pot as he was sure-nuff
card-sharking and letting everybody know
he ain't got to worry about
any bad-teeth motherfuckers jumping
on him, thinking he's not strapped,
so the big maybe is—does he,
shut your mouth,
really have a gun?

Hankering

I'd left the radio on and J.D. McCloud
is playing a Mississippi flood song—
you know, the river that floods every year
under a heavy rain. There is that bluesy
threat of landslides and falling trees,
the water that always wins.
It makes me think of you. It's beyond
old school; it's a song first played
when record shops had radio stations
midnight broadcasting from Memphis
all cross the South, a red-light slow dance
being delivered by thunder angels
on all-terrain vehicles. The true gospel:
the crack in the road where I live now
with our mythology. We been off and on
so long there is a sacredness about us.
I've always been coming towards you
and finishing my cigarette and cup
of black coffee, keeping the radio on, but
I turn it down, play it low so I can hear
the spirits better. I call to the ju-ju band.
They tell me this is a high-water
moment and by now if we don't

have *a real love thing* then
what we really have is nothing.

His Vision of Laying Waste

A damn depredation: a block
east of the Safeway is where Charlie
from the VA group got robbed
in fucking daylight carrying four
damn bags of groceries: corn flakes,
milk, butter and eggs, a good mess
of collards, enough shrimp and lamb
for a few meals of curry. Charlie likes
to eat and every day he cooks
'cause being in his kitchen don't
make him think 'bout Nam.
He had five pounds of basmati rice,
bacon, a bag of red beans and some
hickory-smoked turkey for seasoning,
bell peppers—red and green,
and a few yellow onions,
the bags dangling close to the ground.
Two teenagers just walk up. Skinny one
is shaking, points the gun
right at Charlie's face—so he slowly
sets the bags down. He can see them both,
the other one is chewing gum.
Charlie done lived war, done run
through jungle being shot at.

Gum-chewer says *give it up asshole,*
so Charlie does. He surprises them,
empties his pockets just like that.
Gum-chewer big-scowls but takes
the money anyway. Shaky-gun,
confused by how easy it all is,
asks him, *what we do now?*
Gum-chewer pauses like he has
to think about it. That's when
Charlie gets scared
and his PTSD kicks in.

Cultivating My No-Regret

I am the age when shoveling snow
can take me out, and as a matter
of fact, right now, I do live in a barn.
Three Douglas fir, sentinels
at the corner of my fence,
reach a hundred feet into morning fog,
two juvenile eagles glide silently
the middle of this northwest world,
the lagoon at high tide, its snags
near the tall trees
where great blue herons build strong
nests lined
with moss and foliage, where crows
address each other and take turns
feeding. A dog who isn't mine loves me
and every morning comes to howl
at my door. I step out and sit with her
on my small porch, watch sunrise over
crests of hills on the inlet's old-growth side,
and this is a prayer, a sacredness
that takes hold of me, and whatever
it was I told you yesterday
about how such longing is pure,
that still counts.

February 26, 2012, the Blood Moon

for Trayvon

I'm a slow old man on the sidewalk,
crown of my ballcap pulled low
over my dome, the complaining crows
that roost on the powerline across
the street are angels in the gloam.
As sure as a hooded sweatshirt
can keep you warm in winter,
the leaned-on car horn heralds
like a newspaper the trauma we fear,
all the way back to the slave ships,
the bloodline. The crows call
to family alive and dead, a dreadful
red moon, the murder of a black boy
in the early evening just living
in his own skin, carrying a bag
of Skittles and a bottle of sweet tea.

To Breathe, May 25, 2020

after George Floyd

To suck air into my nigga lungs
and expel it; the inhale and
exhale that controls my nigga voice,
the stuttered words and the songs
I try to sing; to pause, as for breath
to pant, take a rest; to move gently
or blow lightly; to smell the air
in my mother's flower garden
or her kitchen with bread in the oven;
to absorb oxygen while I sweat
as a result of any exertion; to
be exposed in order to develop
after being uncorked; to live, to be
allowed, as you were not, *to live.*

Collage: Benediction to the Juke-Joint

May the Lord watch between me and thee
Kind words strangers we hope to meet
Scars of a street musician a bundle of choruses
Radio station theme songs and badlands jingles
Selections of less-than-holy incantations
Living in the land of the cottonmouths
Unmitigated trauma the water in the lungs
Cardiac arrest an immutable correlation
Last call at the Uptown Bar and Grill
Victims are always nostalgia-free
A pandemic of vacant theaters
May the Lord watch between me and thee
While we're absent one from another

Wife.Beater

*

He's a galaxy, he's a planet,
he's a solar system—
everything revolves around him.
It's his car, his money
in the bank, his house is his fucking castle,
he's the king, the dog,
he's big-dick-daddy the long stroker,
he knows her missing-tooth smile
beams upward, toward him,
her blacked eye seems to be winking
at him, her pussy is zipped up in his pants.

*

The Old Rule was that the size of the stick
a man could use to beat his wife
could be no bigger than the width of his thumb.
Black men could not beat black women
with impunity because they didn't own them.
They could not whip them any more
than they could unjustly whip the master's horse.
In the South when the war was over
there was no chattel slavery,
and then the marital violence
became a political issue.
To feed their need for free labor
the dubious law that limited the size
of the stick in wife beating was repurposed
and used to arrest black men for their
domestic violence and hold them in jails
to be leased to plantations, enslaved again.

*

My grandfather—a flash
of gold tooth, a drinker,
a gambler because what else
could a one-legged man do,
what other employment
was there for a crippled
high-yellow rounder who
abandoned his wife, a church
woman, a black Cherokee,
daughter of the maroons
with his six children, five boys
and one girl, and the oldest
my father, he was thirteen
and left school, and took a job
a white farmer that knew
this blues story offered him
to slop hogs and drive tractor
in his fields of corn and cotton
because with no man in the house
the family still had to eat
and thc boy's premature
manhood started right there,

and everything he didn't
know about being a man
didn't mean anything
if he could feed his father's
family, his family.

*

The list of things my father never had a chance to do:

1) every teen-age kid thing
2) every teen-age kid thing
3) every teen-age kid thing
4) every teen-age kid thing
5) etc.

*

—her father
had died from pneumonia, her two
older brothers were murdered,
and the youngest boy had been sent
to live with relatives in the safety
of a northern city, so, the man knew
she had no one to protect her.

One Saturday night she was getting ready
to go out dancing with her girlfriends,
he was drunk and did not want her to go.
When she came into the room after her bath
he laid across the bed smirking and smoking
as she went to the closet: she screamed
when she found that he'd cut a big hole
in the back of each one of her party dresses.
He told her, *go 'head, step out, show your black ass*—
that meanness had always been there, long
before he began letting the children see him
put his truck-driving fists to her.

*

The preemptive strike—the hatred
some husbands develop for the wife
without any apparent reason
is maybe because the woman he married
is not the woman he thought
he married; one of those reasons
that only makes sense to another wife-beater;
his idea that the younger woman stands at
a crossroad of domestic mayhem and
possible murder only because she is young
and always trying to overshadow
the husband with her education and better
employment status. But not because
he is also young and therefore might possess
the more vivid shade of violence.
It might be too late for her
when she finally sees the shadow of it:
violence, an old testament he's always had.
Maybe now he has a hidden agenda
as well, something to hide that
the young wife doesn't know about,
maybe he has the classic side-babe

or he's just slinging dick all around
and believes that whatever he's getting
on the outside is something the wife
isn't providing, which means he simply
doesn't have a reason why he's always screwfaced,
just that no human being is perfect, he might say,
but a man that doesn't respect his woman
can find a fault in everything she does,
like maybe she squeezes the tube
of toothpaste in the middle, see,
it's even the little things that can breed
a quarrel and a beating.

*

My father had braided a whip
of five hickory switches and made
my mama strip and lay face down
on the hallway hardwood floor
and he beat her like a white man
beats a slave; she'd been a teenage bride
so pretty, and he thought that he had
effectively run all other available men
away from her—but a boy baby
was born six months after their wedding,
a boy in whom he couldn't find any
of his pecan-brown resemblance
with the baby's indigo color
so further doubt firmly set in.

*

When I was a teenage revolutionary
on the other side of the state
and one of my brothers was also
in the revolution but was incarcerated,
and the youngest brother was slinging
hash, eggs, and coffee at an all-night diner
in a New Jersey tourist town,
my sister, who was a senior in high school
called the sheriffs' office because
she was afraid my father was gonna kill
my mother he was beating her so bad.
But the white man my father drove
long-haul truck for, bringing his bottle
of moonshine, talked with the sheriff,
and my father didn't spend one night
in jail, so he returned to the house
and sawed off the broomstick and beat
my sister with it until she couldn't get up
goddammit calling the law on me!
which made my other two sisters
forever afraid to get involved.
Both married wife-beating husbands.

*

Summer I was five we lived
in Queens and every time
my father came home
I would begin to stutter, as I would
for the next 20 years
until I learned to breathe.

He was the terrorizer.
He was the everlasting winter freeze.

Everyone that knew my father knew
he beat his wife—us children, we
were ashamed, my aunt and the uncles,
my grandmother—they all loved him,
even though ashamed.

*

Drinking in the kitchen alone do you
reckon it was difficult for him
to reconcile with the man he was?
Do you think that he didn't know
he was the monster whenever he had
that green plastic pint bottle of cheap
rot-gut scotch tucked in his ass pocket?
Do you think that he prayed to God to stop
him from beating on her—or were those
the nights God Himself was drunk?

*

If any society, a red state or a blue state,
any county, any neighborhood
or community on a dirt road, if that place
depends on physical force
to uphold any law, especially where
there is no sexual equality—
then I can fucking guarantee you are living
in a country, a neighborhood, or
on the dirt road where wife-beating
is a reflection of the societal violence
that gets ignored; one night
my father threw bricks
through the glass of every window—
starting with the master bedroom
where my mother was fearfully
sleeping after she'd locked the doors
so she wouldn't get beaten.

*

I've never been a boy afraid to fight, nor
a hand-shy dog who whimpered, backing away
with my tail tucked, so when at nineteen
I came home to visit my grandma after
my 30 days for drunk and disorderly—
I was in her kitchen drinking sassafras tea
feeling good by the woodstove.
My father showed up and eventually
slapped me across my mouth because
I had a difference of political opinion.
Before he could pull his right hand back
to do it again I had put my fist in the middle
of his face and loosened some of his teeth,
ooohh he says *so you gonna fight me like*
you a man uhh, and he came at me again
and we went through MamaDaisy's screen door
and off her porch into the yard where
he landed on top and knocked the wind
out of me; then he reached into his back pocket
and pulled out the pistol, and I knew
this was something that had been living,
breathing within him. My grandmother

had come down into the yard wailing.
Aunt Ida, her sister who lived across
the weed-choked field, heard her and
came on the run, and those two old women
who'd had a lifetime of begging knew
how to beg that gun out of my father's hand.
They saved me, and we watched him
drive away squealing down the blacktop.

*

It was a Wednesday in the January ice
that I rode the bus three hours,
from Winston-Salem to Hertford,
and then since I, being black, couldn't sit
in the warm comfort at the counter
inside the bus terminal, I used the payphone
outside the station to call Herman
in Sandy Cross to come pick me up
and drive me to the house. I needed
to see my people, and it being the middle
of the week, I knew most likely
my father would be on the road, maybe
at a truck stop coming off some highway
up in the mountains, probably in the sleeper cab
of his Mack with some bar gal he'd met
in a roadhouse where he was probably
playing Etta James' *I'd rather go blind*
than see you walk away, his theme song
for any woman that happens along.

*

I walked into the cold house
where my mother lived
under my father's roof; the unlit furnace
made it seem even colder and my mother
said it was because he didn't leave
money to keep the furnace on
and all she had was his $400 check
that had come in the mail, did I think
I could *go to James Edwards' store*
and cash it for 10 dollars of heating oil?
It was so cold that James Edwards
didn't give one-white-man-thought
about not cashing it. I drove back
to the house, poured the oil
into the tank, lit the pilot
and the radiant fire anointed
the house. I handed the remaining
cash from the check to my mother.

*

My father came home early and found out
I had cashed his check,
got pissed, asked me for the rest of the money,
the cash I had given over to my mother,
and she said she'd spent it all
on groceries and bills and whatever else
my little brother and two sisters needed.
My father then called the sheriff and claimed
I had forged and cashed his $400 check,
which technically I had, and he took off
to Miss Morris' liquor house fussing and
fuming about my mother and me.
I knew it was gonna take 30 minutes
for the deputy sheriff across county
to get to the house, and that was
all the time I needed; my mother
made a phone call to get me a ride
and packed cold fried chicken
to carry me down the road.

*

(There is an unspoken legitimacy of intrafamily
violence in all cultures according to authorities
on such things. It's the what-happens-inside-
our-doors-stays-inside-our-doors decree.
Roll the laugh track, it's *The Honeymooners*,
it's Ralph's balled-fist threat to send Alice
to the moon, to the moon Alice, to the moon.
The home is the setting in which most of us
first experience physical violence.
The term *wifebeater* is unthinkably used
to describe the sleeveless ribbed undershirt
that Stanley wore on the desirable streetcar
and which has now become the symbol
which points to the seen-but-not-seen
behavior of men who bash their women—
the battering of women by husbands, ex-husbands,
or lovers being the major cause of injuries
to American women.)

*

He made the mistake of attacking her
in the kitchen, and because his dinner
was late he slapped her from the stove
to the counter to teach her a lesson,
knocked pots still cooking to the floor,
he broke dishes, scattered utensils, cornered
her by the cabinet above the butcher
block with its assortment of knives—
she grabbed the first one she could reach
and drove it into his chest,

and that stopped everything—

he dropped into a chair at the table where
my cousin Lil' Mike had also been waiting
on dinner. My father was trying to control
his breathing and pretty as you please
asked my mother to drive him the thirty miles
to the next county's hospital and it seemed
the knife was still vibrating when she said
he could fucking drive himself. Later he told
his brother he would've bled to death

if he had pulled the blade out, so he didn't,
but with every turn of the steering wheel
the blade cut him a little deeper.

Coda

1.

When my mother called and told me
she was going to remarry my father,
and because it somehow signaled that he
was also on the phone listening,
I incredulously asked, *what exactly is it*
about your marriage that y'all don't remember?

2.

Some years after their second, and final, divorce,
we're at a family holiday at my brother's house,
my mother announces that she was grateful
to be in our presence with the love of her life;
she was talking about Mr. McCoy just beaming
beside her. They were styling, color-coordinated,
I knew what that meant, and how much she enjoyed it.
But even as my father was into his third marriage
and sitting there with his second wife, I could see

from the tightening in his jaw that
her statement stung him.

3.

I was smoking under the eaves on
the backyard deck in soft summer rain,
back when I still smoked cigarettes:
my father walked out from the kitchen
pulling his necessary mobile canister
of oxygen as he coughed a conspiratorial beg
for one of my Marlboros. I told him, *take two.*

We had come to an agreement that if he stopped
disrespecting me every chance he could get
at our family gatherings that I would never do
anything to show his grandchildren what kind
of asshole he was, because I realized
he was giving his grandkids a much better
experience than he had ever given me.
It showed that he loved them, and they
loved him back because of it and
I would never take that away from them.

He shook my hand on it and called me *son*
and I told him I thought that was a bit much.
But from that day forward he continued
to address me as *son*. And this became our truce.

4.

On one of the last days that I would ever
be with my mother I apologized
and said to her I'm sorry that when I was a kid
I could not protect her, knowing full-well
why those beatings were happening.
Her apology to me was a surprise
of how it hurt her that she could not ever
protect me from him, and I was there
beside her bed, a silent weeping in my indigo,
her hand in God's hand, my hand in hers.

Acknowledgements

To my family extended, my grands, my aunties and uncles, my nephews and nieces, and all the cousins who loved and supported me through everything, for ancestors known and unknown, I could not have made it without you all.

Thank you, Marcella Lilley-Ricks, for your love and timely strength when I needed it most, much love.

To my good friends who inspired me and helped me through this work in so many ways: Kim Addonizio, Danny Caron, Tess Gallagher, Terrance Hayes, Sam Ligon, and John Riley.

For roots, the Black Rooster Collective: Brandon Johnson, Ernesto Mercer, Joel Diaz-Porter, and Renee Stout.

Various versions of several of these poems first appeared in *Five Points*.

My gratitude to Four Way Books.

To Tess, for the love of me and my poetry.

About the Author

Gary Copeland Lilley, originally from North Carolina, now lives in the Pacific Northwest. He has published nine books of poetry, and has appeared in numerous anthologies and journals. Lilley has received the Washington DC Commission on the Arts Fellowship for Poetry and is a graduate of the Warren Wilson College MFA Program for Writers. He teaches in the Western Colorado University Creative Writing MFA program. Lilley serves as the Artistic Director of the Port Townsend Writers Conference and is a Cave Canem Fellow.

We are also grateful to those individuals who participated in our Build a Book Program. They are:

Anonymous (5), Robert Abrams, Debra Allbery, Maggie Anderson, Jean Ball, Sally Ball, Adria Bernardi, Richard Blanchard, Laurel Blossom, Lee Briccetti, Anne Babson Carter, Jennifer Christman, Aaron Coleman, Peter Coyote, Elinor Cramer, Michael Anna de Armas, Brian Komei Dempster, Patrick Donnelly, Lynn Emanuel, Joan Frank, Rigoberto Gonzalez, Elizabeth T. Gray Jr., David and Joan Grubin, Naomi Guttman and Jonathan Mead, Beth Harrison, Jeffrey Harrison, KT Herr, Carlie Hoffman, Elizabeth Jackson, Linda Susan Jackson, Marilyn Johnson, Deborah Jonas-Walsh, Maeve Kinkead, David Lee and Jamila Trindle, Rodney Terich Leonard, Jen Levitt, Howard Levy, Owen Lewis and Susan Ennis, Ralph and Mary Ann Lowen, Maja Lukic, Ricardo Alberto Maldonado, Cleopatra Mathis, Victoria McCoy, Lupe Mendez, Mary Jane Nealon, Nicole Nevadunsky, Kimberly Nunes, Cathy McArthur Palermo, Veronica Patterson, Eileen Pollack, Martha Rhodes, Soraya Shalforoosh, Sarah Stone, Yerra Sugarman, Marjorie and Lew Tesser, Reed Turchi, Maria Walsh, and Calvin Wei